BLAZERS

TO THE EXTREME

Downhill BMX

by Sarah L. Schuette

Reading Consultant:
Barbara J. Fox
Reading Specialist
North Carolina State University

Capstone *press*

Mankato, Minnesota

Blazers is published by Capstone Press,
151 Good Counsel Drive, P.O. Box 669, Mankato, Minnesota 56002.
www.capstonepub.com

Printed in the United States of America in Stevens Point, Wisconsin.
032010
005744R

Library of Congress Cataloging-in-Publication Data
Schuette, Sarah L., 1976–
    Downhill BMX / by Sarah L. Schuette.
    p. cm.—(Blazers—to the extreme)
    Includes bibliographical references and index.
    ISBN-13: 978-0-7368-3785-9 (hardcover)
    ISBN-10: 0-7368-3785-X (hardcover)
    ISBN-13: 978-0-7368-5220-3 (softcover pbk.)
    ISBN-10: 0-7368-5220-4 (softcover pbk.)
    1. Bicycle motocross—Juvenile literature. I. Title. II. Series.
GV1049.3.S35 2005
796.6'2—dc22   2004018353

Summary: Describes the sport of downhill BMX, including bike and
    safety information.

Credits
Jason Knudson, set designer; Enoch Peterson, book designer;
    Kelly Garvin, photo researcher; Scott Thoms, photo editor

Photo Credits
SportsChrome Inc., cover; Tom DiPace, 22–23
Transworld BMX/Keith Mulligan, 4–5, 6, 7, 8–9, 10–11, 12–13, 14,
    15, 16, 17, 18–19, 21, 24–25, 26, 27, 28–29

Table of Contents

The Race Begins

A group of downhill BMX racers
speed down the starting ramp.
The 40-second race begins.

Ramp

The riders reach the first turn. Each turn is called a berm. One rider takes the lead. He pulls ahead of the group.

Berm

The leader gets close to the finish line. He flies over the last jump. He lands perfectly and finishes first.

BLAZER FACT

Each BMX race is called a moto.

Watch the Gate

Before each race, riders balance
their bikes on the starting gate.
They stand on the pedals waiting
for the signal to start.

Up to eight riders compete in each race. Downhill BMX tracks have many jumps, berms, and clear areas.

BLAZER FACT

Downhill BMX riders do not do tricks.

Around each berm, riders choose their lanes. Some move to the top of the curve. Others stay at the bottom of the curve to pass.

Jumps along the course challenge riders. Riders keep looking forward to see the next jump.

BMX Bikes

Downhill BMX bikes take a beating. Riders land hard after jumps. Steel frames help make the bikes sturdy.

Wide, knobby tires help with traction. The tire treads grab the dirt track. Good tires keep racers from slipping on the dirt.

BLAZER FACT

Riders cannot touch each other during a race.

Downhill BMX Diagram

Knobby tires

Helmet

Gloves

Frame

Riding Safely

Riders wear gloves and helmets to stay safe. They wear pads under their jerseys and long pants for more protection.

Riders bend their arms and legs before landing a jump. They try to crouch low to avoid getting hurt during a crash.

Racers ready!

Glossary

berm (BURM)—a banked turn or corner on a downhill BMX track

frame (FRAYM)—the main body of a BMX bike

traction (TRAK-shuhn)—the gripping power that keeps a moving body from slipping on a surface

tread (TRED)—the ridges on a tire

Read More

Firestone, Mary. *Extreme Downhill BMX Moves.* Behind the Moves. Mankato, Minn.: Capstone Press, 2004.

Mahaney, Ian F. *Dave Mirra: BMX Champion.* Extreme Sports Biographies. New York: Rosen, 2005.

Partland, J. P., and Tony Donaldson. *The World of BMX.* Enthusiast Color Series. St. Paul, Minn.: MBI, 2003.

Internet Sites

FactHound offers a safe, fun way to find Internet sites related to this book. All of the sites on FactHound have been researched by our staff.

Here's how:

1. Visit *www.facthound.com*
2. Type in this special code **073683785X** for age-appropriate sites. Or enter a search word related to this book for a more general search.
3. Click on the **Fetch It** button.

FactHound will fetch the best sites for you!

Index